A NOTE TO PARENTS

When your children are ready to "step into reading," giving them the right books—and lots of them—is as crucial as giving them the right food to eat. **Step into Reading Books** present exciting stories and information reinforced with lively, colorful illustrations that make learning to read fun, satisfying, and worthwhile. They are priced so that acquiring an entire library of them is affordable. And they are beginning readers with an important difference—they're written on four levels.

Step 1 Books, with their very large type and extremely simple vocabulary, have been created for the very youngest readers. **Step 2 Books** are both longer and slightly more difficult. **Step 3 Books,** written to mid-second-grade reading levels, are for the child who has acquired even greater reading skills. **Step 4 Books** offer exciting nonfiction for the increasingly proficient reader.

Children develop at different ages. **Step into Reading Books,** with their four levels of reading, are designed to help children become good—and interested—readers *faster*. The grade levels assigned to the four steps—preschool through grade 1 for Step 1, grades 1 through 3 for Step 2, grades 2 and 3 for Step 3, and grades 2 through 4 for Step 4—are intended only as guides. Some children move through all four steps very rapidly; others climb the steps over a period of several years. These books will help your child "step into reading" in style!

1260 1066

(2)

*To R. C., my companion in baseball
and the rest of life
—S. A. K.*

*To my children, Scott, Megan,
Jamie, Chris, and Brandon
—J. C.*

Photo Credits: Focus on Sports: cover (lower left), pp. 39, 44; National Baseball Library, Cooperstown, N.Y.: cover (upper left, lower right, lower center), pp. 11, 12, 19, 20, 25, 29; Ken Regan/Camera 5: cover (upper right), pp. 35, 36; Mitchell B. Reibel/Fotosport: p. 42; UPI/Bettmann Newsphotos: pp. 33, 41.

Library of Congress Cataloging-in-Publication Data
Kramer, Sydelle.
 Baseball's greatest pitchers / by S. A. Kramer ; illustrated by Jim Campbell.
  p. cm. — (Step into reading. A Step 4 book)
 Summary: Relates the stories of five outstanding baseball pitchers, from Walter Johnson to Nolan Ryan.
 ISBN 0-679-82149-X (trade). — ISBN 0-679-92149-4 (lib. bdg.)
 1. Pitchers (Baseball)—United States—Biography—Juvenile literature. [1. Baseball players. 2. Baseball—History.]
I. Campbell, Jim, ill. II. Title. III. Series: Step into reading.
Step 4 book. GV865.A1K73 1992 796.357′092′2—dc20 [B] 91-27892

Manufactured in the United States of America 10 9 8 7 6 5 4 3 2 1

STEP INTO READING is a trademark of Random House, Inc.

Step into Reading

BASEBALL'S GREATEST P·I·T·C·H·E·R·S

By S. A. Kramer
Illustrated by Jim Campbell

A Step into Sports Step 4 Book

Random House 🏠 New York

A Note to the Reader

If you ever want to start an argument, just ask a bunch of baseball fans to name the greatest pitchers of all time. They'll never agree!

Out of the hundreds and hundreds of pitchers who have played major-league baseball, only about 50 are in the Hall of Fame. And just 15 of those pitchers have won 300 or more games. That's not a big group to choose from. Still, it's hard to say who the greatest are.

But a few make it onto nearly everyone's list. They're the ones who performed great feats year after year. They were legends in their own time, and they're legends today. Read about them—and be amazed!

1

The Nice Guy

Weiser, Idaho. 1907.

Another swing and a miss! The young pitcher with the blazing fastball is striking everyone out. In the stands a traveling salesman watches, amazed. It's not the majors—this boy is pitching for the local phone company. But that makes no difference to the salesman. He's sure he's watching the fastest pitcher anywhere!

The salesman writes a letter to a major-league team called the Washington Nationals. He claims he's found the world's greatest pitcher—a nineteen-year-old farmboy named Walter Johnson who "throws a ball so fast it's like a little white bullet."

The Nationals' manager doesn't believe the letter, but he wants to help his losing team. So he sends a scout to Idaho. When the scout sees Walter fire his fastball, he grabs a piece of brown wrapping paper and quickly scribbles out a contract. Walter doesn't sign it until his father gives his permission. Then he hurries to Washington.

Walter's never been East before. He's a country boy, and he feels nervous about the big city. He wonders if he's really good enough to play in the major leagues.

When he arrives at the ballpark, his teammates are waiting. They see a tall, shy teenager who blushes easily. They can tell Walter isn't used to dressing up. His pants are too short, his sleeves are too long, and his hat is too small. But he has an honest face and a friendly smile.

That day the Nationals must play a tough team, the Detroit Tigers. Walter takes the mound for his first major-league start.

The Tigers have heard about this farmboy with a fastball, but when they watch Walter warm up, they're sure they can beat him. His motion is so relaxed they figure he can't be throwing that hard. Plus, he looks clumsy because his arms seem too long for his body.

Just before the game starts, some of the Tigers start mooing like cows. Others begin to holler from the bench. But Walter ignores them.

The first batter comes up. Walter's windup is short. He flings his long right arm back so far the batter can see the ball. He comes around sidearm, so low it's nearly underhand. When he releases the pitch, it's as though he's snapped a whip.

The Tigers stop laughing. They can't get a hit. Pitches whiz by so fast they can hear but not see them. Their best player, Ty Cobb, says the ball "hisses with danger." It moves so quickly some can't swing and have to bunt instead. By the time the game ends, Walter has proved he belongs in the big leagues.

For the next twenty years Walter's fastball roars by batters. To a right-handed hitter, it tails in and sinks; to a left-handed hitter, it breaks away and dips. It's so powerful that some players don't want to bat against him. When their teams face Walter, they pretend to be sick.

One day Walter pitches against the

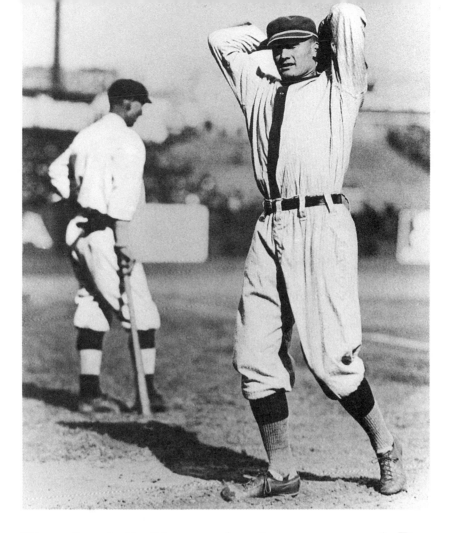

Cleveland Indians. A player named Ray Chapman comes to the plate. Walter's first two pitches are so fast Ray can't even swing the bat. He tosses it away and heads toward the bench. The umpire calls out, "That's only strike two." Ray shouts over his shoulder, "I know it. You can have the next one. It won't do me any good."

Most people think Walter is baseball's greatest pitcher. But he's also known as one of the game's best sports. He tried never to hit batters, since he feared his fastball would hurt them. And if he accidentally did, he'd help them up. He comforted his teammates if they made errors—even if those errors cost him the game. When his team was ahead, he'd let friends and rookies get hits. Ballplayers loved him, and so did the fans.

There's an old saying: Nice guys finish last. It sure wasn't true about Walter Johnson.

WALTER PERRY JOHNSON
(The Big Train, Barney)

1887–1946

6'1", 200 lb.

Right-handed

Pitching career: 1907–27

Games won: 416 (2nd)*

Games lost: 279 (3rd)*

ERA: 2.17 (7th)*†

Strikeouts: 3,508 (7th)*

Shutouts: 110 (1st)*

• Great Feats •

• Won twenty or more games twelve times, including ten years in a row.

• Led the American League in strikeouts twelve times, including eight years in a row.

• Was 36–7 in 1913, with an ERA of 1.09.

• Eleven seasons with an ERA under 2.00.

• Pitched the most shutouts ever (110).

• Tied for most victories in a row (American League): sixteen.

• Was one of the first five players to be elected to the Hall of Fame.

• Greatest Feat •

• Pitched three shutouts against the New York Yankees in four days, allowing a total of just nine hits (1908).

*Shows all-time rank among major-league players.

†ERA (earned run average): The average number of earned runs a pitcher has allowed for every nine innings he has pitched.

2

The Sore Loser

Lefty Grove smashes his fist into his locker. Lefty's angry—*very* angry. He and his team, the Philadelphia Athletics, have just lost a close one, 1–0.

Lefty has never wanted to win so badly. It's 1931, and a victory would have earned him a new major-league record: seventeen wins in a row.

Lefty can't stop thinking about it. Suddenly, he rips his shirt so hard the buttons sail across the room. He reaches out and tears his locker right out of the wall. Then he starts to wreck the whole room.

He yanks another locker out, and then another, and another. Bats begin flying, and balls and gloves and shoes. He lifts benches as though they were pillows and

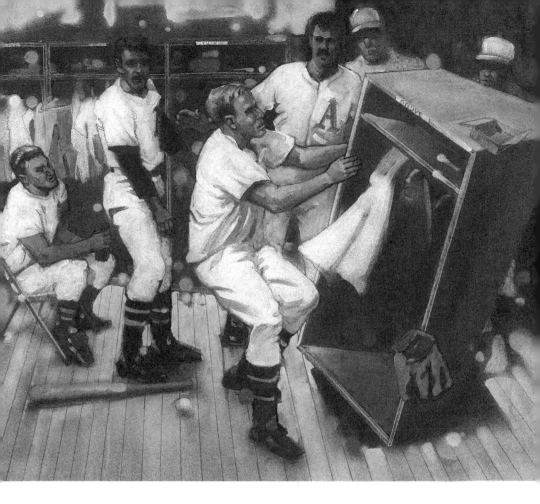

smashes them on the ground.

Lefty's teammates just watch. They aren't surprised. Lefty is famous for his terrible temper. When he loses a close game, he often flies into a rage. But the players know he's never totally out of control. How do they know? He'll smack his right hand into anything—but never his left. He saves that hand for pitching only.

Lefty doesn't leave his temper in the locker room. He's a terror on the field as well. He'll throw at batters to keep them from crowding the plate. He never hits them in the head, but he'll whip his deadly fastball in right under their chin. He sometimes even throws at his teammates during batting practice! If someone gets upset, he'll stand on the mound and laugh.

The men admire Lefty as a player anyway. No one wants to win more. He says, "I'm a serious man, and baseball is a serious business." They know he's just about the toughest player in the game.

Lefty's childhood made him tough. His family was very poor, and he left school to support them. At thirteen he was a coal miner. Then he fixed steam engines for the railroad. That was when he started pitching for a local team.

A minor-league manager spotted Lefty and signed him up. He pitched well for years—until he arrived in the majors. Suddenly, Lefty forgot how to throw strikes. His fastball was blazing, but he averaged almost six walks a game.

But Lefty wouldn't be beaten. After a difficult rookie year, he settled down. Then his fastball made him the greatest left-hander ever. He "threw so hard," one batter said, "you wondered the cover didn't fly off the ball." His fastball didn't tail away or in—it didn't have time to. Often it crossed the plate five inches above the batter's swing. It shot home so quickly that not even the catcher knew where it was heading.

In the years Lefty played, no one pitched faster or harder. He never tried to fool the hitters—he just threw the ball right by them. In a tight spot he could pitch even if he'd barely warmed up.

Once Lefty was watching a game from the bench. The Athletics were easily beating the Yankees. But in the ninth the Yanks suddenly filled the bases with no outs. The A's had to make a pitching change. All eyes flashed to the bullpen.

But the manager nodded toward the dugout. Even if Lefty wasn't warmed up, he was the only man for this job. Lefty strolled onto the field. He threw just five warmup pitches—and struck out the side.

Nothing could stop Lefty when he decided to do something. He refused to retire until he'd won his 300th game. And when the American League chose its very first Most Valuable Player, it gave that honor to Lefty Grove.

ROBERT MOSES GROVE
(Lefty, Mose)

1900–75	Games won: 300
6′3″, 190 lb.	Games lost: 141
Left-handed	ERA: 3.06
Pitching career: 1925–41	Strikeouts: 2,266
	Shutouts: 35

• Great Feats •

• Led the American League in ERA nine times (more than anyone else in major-league history), including four years in a row.

• Led the American League in strikeouts seven years in a row.

• Was 31–4 in 1931, with an ERA of 2.06. No pitcher has ever won so many games in a single season while losing so few.

• Won twenty or more games eight times.

• Was elected to the Hall of Fame in 1947.

• Greatest Feat •

• Tied the American League record for sixteen wins in a row (1931).

3

The Oldest Rookie

It's 1965 in Kansas City. The Athletics take the field. All eyes fix on the pitcher. His name is LeRoy Robert "Satchel" Paige. He is an all-time great—but he hasn't thrown in many years. Now he's fifty-nine years old. No one near his age has ever pitched in a major-league game.

Satchel is on the mound because the Athletics know the fans will flock to see him. But this is no exhibition game. It's the real thing. And Satchel will face the hard-hitting Boston Red Sox.

The first batter comes up. The crowd whirs with excitement as the ball zips over the plate. The old man can still pitch!

Three innings later, Satchel comes out of the game. He's given up just one hit. The Red Sox have been held scoreless!

This isn't the first time Satchel Paige
has made baseball history. From 1927 to
1947 he pitched nearly 2,500 games. He
won about 2,000, with 250 shutouts and 45
no-hitters. Once he appeared in 164 games
in a row. In one game he struck out 22
batters. Experts agree he was one of the
greatest pitchers ever.

Yet if you look in the record books, Satchel's name is hardly mentioned. That's because the men who ran baseball before 1947 wouldn't let Satchel pitch for them. Satchel was black, and blacks weren't allowed in the major leagues.

Black athletes like Satchel refused to let that stop them. They formed all-black leagues. Satchel played for many black teams. He also had his own club, Satchel Paige's All-Stars. In the off-season his team played against major leaguers.

People jammed the ballparks to see Satchel pitch. Advertisements read "Satchel Paige, World's Greatest Pitcher." He was "Guaranteed to Strike Out the First Nine Men."

In 1935 something incredible happened. In the last inning of a game, fans booed and made Satchel mad. He stared in at his catcher. Then he threw three fastballs and struck the first batter out.

As the second hitter walked to the plate, Satchel called to his outfielders and waved them into the dugout. The fans were amazed. Satchel hurled three more fastballs–the second batter struck out.

Then Satchel turned to his infield. He waved *them* in too! The players looked at each other and slowly walked off.

The diamond was empty. The crowd grew quiet.

Satchel threw just three pitches. Three

strikes blazed over the plate! He hadn't needed any fielders. The stands shook as the fans roared.

Satchel hardly looked like a great pitcher. His legs were so skinny that his pants flapped in the breeze. He ran like a turkey. And his motion was stiff—as if the Tin Man were on the mound.

Yet the ball did exactly what Satchel wanted it to do. He had spectacular control. He taught himself to place the ball

by throwing over bottle tops. Often, he'd pitch over matchbooks when warming up.

Satchel could do it all. He threw overhand, sidearm, even underhand. He tossed change-ups, curves, knuckleballs, and different kinds of fastballs. He called one sort the "be" ball—"'cause it be where I want it to be." Another was the "thoughtful stuff"—it gave hitters plenty to think about.

In spite of his talent, Satchel thought he'd never play in the majors. But a young black man named Jackie Robinson joined the Brooklyn Dodgers in 1947, and opened baseball to players of all races.

The owner of the Cleveland Indians wanted to sign Satchel up. But the manager was worried. At forty-two, wasn't Satchel too old to pitch?

Satchel agreed to a tryout. "Here's the plate," the manager told him. "See if you can get it up here."

Satchel threw fifty pitches, and forty-six were in the strike zone. Few pitchers of *any* age could duplicate that!

Satchel went on to become the oldest rookie ever. He was even nominated for Rookie of the Year. In 1952, when he was forty-six, he was voted an American League All-Star. And even though he had been kept out of the majors for so many years, baseball recognized his greatness by electing him to the Hall of Fame.

4

The Quiet Hero

The Dodgers have to win this game. It's the only way to stay in the tight 1965 National League pennant race. But they've had only one hit all night. They're leading 1–0, all because of their star pitcher, Sandy Koufax. Now it's the top of the eighth. Can Sandy shut the Cubs down?

He faces three men in this inning: he strikes out all three. The 29,000 fans in Dodger Stadium start to get nervous. Sandy has now retired twenty-four men in a row. Not a single hitter has reached base. Sandy's not just pitching a no-hitter—he might hurl a perfect game!

The ninth inning starts. Sandy walks slowly to the mound. He takes his warm-up tosses. The fans in the ballpark watch his every move.

Sandy strikes the first batter out. He strikes out the second one too. A hush falls over the stadium. The third batter stands at the plate. Sandy goes into his windup, with its slight rocking motion. His arm comes straight down over his head. He's careful to keep his wrist loose as his hand snaps the ball. Strike one!

Sandy winds again. He throws the ball so hard his cap flies off his head. The pitch sails high, and the catcher barely snags it.

Now Sandy leans in and gets the sign. He frowns and grits his teeth as he pitches. Ball two!

Sandy tries to stay calm. He steps off the mound, mops his sweaty forehead, and wipes a finger on his pants.

The batter is waiting. In comes Sandy's pitch. The batter thinks he can hit it—but he swings and misses!

Everyone in the stadium is staring at the mound. The next pitch could win the game and make baseball history.

Sandy goes into his windup. The pitch comes whipping in. Strike three! The crowd is on its feet, roaring its congratulations.

It's September 9, 1965, and Sandy has his perfect game—only the second one in the National League in this century.

The Dodgers go on to win the pennant and the World Series. Their most outstanding player is Sandy Koufax.

Sandy never thought he'd be a baseball player. In fact, he'd won a basketball scholarship to college. After graduation, he planned to be an architect.

But the summer he was nineteen, this

quiet Jewish boy played for a local team in Brooklyn, New York. A Dodger scout was impressed by his fastball. When Sandy signed the contract, he hadn't pitched in more than sixteen games in his whole life!

That turned out to be a big problem. Sandy wasn't ready for the big leagues, but his contract didn't allow him to go to the minors. So he spent the first six years of his career just learning how to pitch. Those years were so hard that he almost quit. Anxious and tense, he was often unable to throw strikes. Even in practice he was so wild that at times he'd miss the batting cage.

Finally, Sandy realized what was wrong. He was trying *too* hard. So he relaxed, and stopped overthrowing. Just before a game, he'd swing like a monkey from the roof of the dugout in order to keep his muscles loose. Soon he was able to put the ball exactly where he wanted it.

For the next five years Sandy was as unbeatable as a pitcher could be. His steaming fastball hopped; his great curveball dove. No one could tell which was coming—he threw them the same way.

Sandy was shy and serious, and kept to himself. But Dodger fans loved him—they packed the stadium when he was pitching.

Then something went wrong with his arm. To kill the pain, he'd get shots. After his starts, he'd soak his arm in ice water. Then he'd coat it with lotion that burned the skin. The next day it would swell and sound like "a soggy sponge." He couldn't even lift it to comb his hair.

Back then doctors didn't know how to treat injuries like this. So Sandy had to retire when he was only thirty years old. That's why some pitchers have better career records—but when Sandy was in top form, no one was greater.

SANFORD KOUFAX
(Sandy)

1935–

6'2", 210 lb.

Left-handed (pitching)

Right-handed (batting)

Pitching career: 1955–66

Games won: 165

Games lost: 87

ERA: 2.76

Strikeouts: 2,396

Shutouts: 40

• Great Feats •

• Led the National League in ERA five years in a row.

• Led the National League in strikeouts four times.

• Was 26–8 in 1965, with an ERA of 2.04 and 382 strikeouts (second highest total in major-league history).

• Pitched four no-hitters in four years, including one perfect game.

• Was elected to the Hall of Fame in 1972.

• Twice won the World Series Most Valuable Player Award.

• Had an ERA of 0.95 in four Series, and 61 strikeouts in 57 innings.

• Won the Cy Young Award three times in four years (when only one award was given for both leagues).

• Won the National League Most Valuable Player Award (1963).

• Greatest Feat •

• Between 1963 and 1966 had a record of 97-27, with 1,228 strikeouts–the four most remarkable pitching years in a row.

5

The Strikeout King

It's hot in the stadium at Anaheim, California, on this August day in 1974. Yet the Angel fans ignore the heat. Nolan Ryan smokes his fastball past one Detroit Tiger after another. He winds, kicks his left leg high, and grunts loudly as he delivers. Each pitch travels with amazing speed.

Something out of the ordinary is also happening in the stands. Two engineers sit in the press box above the field. They're there to "clock" Nolan's pitches. Like police radar checking the pace of a passing car, their instruments will measure the exact speed of Nolan's ball. Nolan is fast, but just how fast nobody knows.

Nolan goes into his motion. He's about to fire another fastball. The men get their

instruments ready. The crowd roars with excitement. When Nolan releases the ball, the radar tracks it to the plate.

Something must be wrong. His time is 100.9! Can Nolan really have hurled a ball more than 100 miles per hour? No one has ever been clocked at that speed.

The men measure Nolan's pitches for the rest of the game. He strikes out nineteen batters—and hurls *another* 100.9-mile-per-hour fastball.

It's official. The radar was right. Nolan Ryan has thrown the fastest fastball ever measured. His record is entered into the *Guinness Book of World Records*. No other pitcher has matched it, much less beat it.

Throughout his career Nolan has set other records too. No one's struck out more batters in one season, or over an entire career. He holds nineteen different strikeout records, and is baseball's hardest pitcher to hit. He's pitched more no-hitters

than anyone—seven. In one year, he threw two.

What makes Nolan so difficult to hit? His fastball races in so quickly it explodes over the plate. An umpire once described it as a million blinding specks of white. One batter said, "If he hits you with it, you're dead."

But Nolan throws more than fastballs. He says, "You can't win with one pitch." He has a great curve and a change-up. No one can tell which is coming. Even the kind of pitches that others throw slowly Nolan throws fast: his change-up crosses the plate at 88 miles per hour.

Yet Nolan Ryan isn't unbeatable. He sometimes loses his control. He's walked more batters than anyone else, and has often unleashed wild pitches. He's won more than 300 games, but he has also lost more than 200.

Still, Nolan believes his wildness actually helps him. If a batter's not sure where the ball is heading, he will often get frightened. According to Nolan, "It helps if the hitter thinks you're a little crazy."

For a pitcher, Nolan has had a very long career. He's pitched his way through a quarter of a century. How does Nolan do it? He lifts 100-pound weights with his legs. He rides his exercise bicycle after every game. And he's got some special tricks—he cures his sore fingers by soaking them in pickle juice!

Nolan Ryan's more than just a great pitcher. Most people think he's one of the finest men in the game. Even in difficult situations, he's always polite. He's so popular with his teammates, ten of them have named their sons after him.

When Nolan was a boy, his hero was Sandy Koufax. Nolan never guessed that one day he would be a hero for the pitchers of tomorrow.

LYNN NOLAN RYAN
(The Express)

1947–

6′2″, 210 lb.

Right-handed

Pitching career: 1966–

Games won: 314*

Games lost: 278* (4th)

ERA: 3.16*

Strikeouts: 5,511* (1st)

Shutouts: 61* (tied for 7th)

• Great Feats •

• Has led the league in strikeouts eleven times, including six seasons in which he struck out more than 300.

• Holds the strikeout record for a single season (383), 1973.

• Has pitched seven no-hitters, the most in major-league history, including two in one season (1973).

• Averaged 11.48 strikeouts per nine innings in 1987, the highest in major-league history.

• Hardest pitcher to get a hit off in baseball history.

• Greatest Feat •

• Struck out nineteen batters in a game twice in one year (1974).

*As of the end of 1991.

6
More Greats

Johnson, Grove, Paige, Koufax, Ryan: all fans would agree they're among baseball's greatest hurlers. Who are some other greats? Here are a few.

Denton True Young was better known as Cy (short for Cyclone, since he once threw a ball so hard it broke some boards off the stands). Baseball named its pitching award after him. Why? He was probably the greatest control pitcher ever, winning more games (511) than any other major leaguer. It's the one pitching record that experts think will never be broken. *Pitching career:* 1890–1911.

Grover Cleveland Alexander is second in shutouts (90) and tied for third in games won (373). He had amazing control, and hated to waste pitches. He once got twelve men out in four innings on just twelve pitches! He also hurled an entire game in 58 minutes. *Pitching career:* 1911–30.

Christy Mathewson is tied for third in games won (373) and is third in shutouts (80). He won more than twenty games a season for twelve straight years. Christy was known for his good manners and education (he was a college graduate at a time when few ballplayers were). He left baseball to join the army during World War I. He was poisoned by gas during the fighting and never really recovered. *Pitching career:* 1900–16.

Bob Gibson had what some consider the greatest season ever. In 1968 he was 22–9, with an ERA of 1.12 (the second lowest ever in the National League). Thirteen of his wins were shutouts (the second highest total ever in a single season), and the teams that faced him averaged fewer than six hits per game. Throughout his career, his fierce glare made batters tremble. He was one of baseball's toughest pitchers—he once hurled an inning despite a broken leg. *Pitching career:* 1959–75.

Tom Seaver was considered modern baseball's most thoughtful pitcher. One manager called him "the smartest pitcher I have ever been around." Hitters felt he was able to read their minds: he hardly ever threw them what they expected. Third in total strikeouts (3,640), he won 311 games. His fastball and slider were so dazzling he once struck out ten men in a row—a record. *Pitching career:* 1967–86.

What about the young pitchers of today? Which of them will make the list of all-time greats? Keep watching and guessing. That's part of the fun of being a fan!